First published in Great Britain in 2024

by NQ Publishers, an imprint of Nextquisite Ltd

Copyright © 2024 by Nextquisite Ltd

All rights reserved. Unauthorised reproduction, in any manner, is prohibited.

www.nqpublishers.com

www.nextquisite.com

Project Director Anne McRae
Art Director Marco Nardi

Illustrations Giulia Lombardo
Text Mary Auld
Picture Research Nicola Burns
Graphic Design Marco Nardi
Layout Design Jeni Child
Consultant: Dr John Haywood

ISBN 978-1-912944-35-4

Printed in China

GREAT CIVILISATIONS

Written by Mary Auld • Illustrated by Giulia Lombardo

NQ PUBLISHERS
For enquiring minds

CONTENTS

Introduction 6

PREHISTORY

The Journey to Civilisation 10
The Birth of Farming 12

AFRICA

Ancient Egypt 16
Ancient Africa 18

ASIA

Mesopotamia 22
The Indus Valley 24
Ancient China 26
Ancient Korea 28
Ancient Japan 30
Southeast Asia 32

EUROPE

The Minoans 36
Ancient Greece 38
The Celts 40
Ancient Rome 42
The Vikings 44

THE AMERICAS

Native Americans 48
Maya and Aztecs 50
The Inca Empire 52

OCEANIA

Ancient Australia 56
Pacific Peoples 58
Glossary 60
Index 63

INTRODUCTION

This book helps you start to explore some of the great ancient civilisations of the world. We have tried to include as many as possible, placing them within geographical regions of the world.

Unique cultures

The word 'civilisation' comes from the Latin word *civitas*, which means city. It was first used to describe cultures that were centred around larger, urban settlements. However, in this book, we use it to talk about groups of people from the past who had strong, unique cultures. Many led settled lives not entirely focused on farming. They made things and traded with each other. These civilisations had structured societies and systems of government, although we do not always know exactly how they worked. Most importantly, these peoples were creating art, developing science and technology, and building monuments. In many cases, they were also writing.

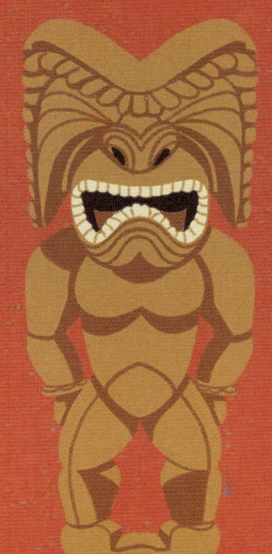

From pre-history to the modern era

To understand how civilisations developed, we need to go back to really 'ancient' human times, known as prehistory, when nothing was written down. The civilisations that followed prehistory are 'ancient', too, in that most of them no longer exist. Some emerge in the late Stone Age, some end with the Medieval Age. But these Ages happened at different times in different parts of the world and some of the civilisations and cultures we discuss still exist today.

We hope you enjoy this first look at ancient civilisations and that it inspires you to find out more about the incredibly rich variety of human history.

Note on dates

Dates in this book are shown as BCE (Before Common Era) and CE (Common Era). The Common Era starts with year 1.

PREH

The word 'prehistory' refers to the period of human history before we had written records. It stretches from at least 2.6 million years ago when our earliest ancestors

STORY

began making and using stone tools, up until about 5,000 years ago when the first writing systems were invented. Writing began independently in the Near East, China and Mesoamerica.

THE JOURNEY TO CIVILISATION

Our earliest ancestors evolved in Africa. They were related to apes but stood more upright. There were different types, or species. Around two million years ago, one species, *Homo erectus*, began to spread into Europe and Asia. *Homo erectus* died out about 100,000 years ago. Modern humans, or *Homo sapiens*, developed in Africa about 300,000 years ago. They migrated from Africa too, gradually settling all over the world.

Making tools

Stone tools found in Africa date back at least 2.6 million years. They show that our early ancestors had developed the intelligence to chip and shape rocks so as to make cutting edges. These tools give their name to this era: the Stone Age.

This handaxe was made by Homo erectus *about 1.6 million years ago.*

Hunters

Our oldest ancestors probably ate meat by scavenging animal remains left behind by predators. But in the Stone Age they became active hunters. Using stone spears, they worked together to kill large animals. And they used tools to skin these animals and cut them up.

The control of fire

We can't say for sure when our ancestors learnt to control fire, but it was probably about a million years ago. Using fire allowed them to cook food, stay warm, scare away predators and live in colder climates.

Human language may have developed as hunters worked together to catch their prey.

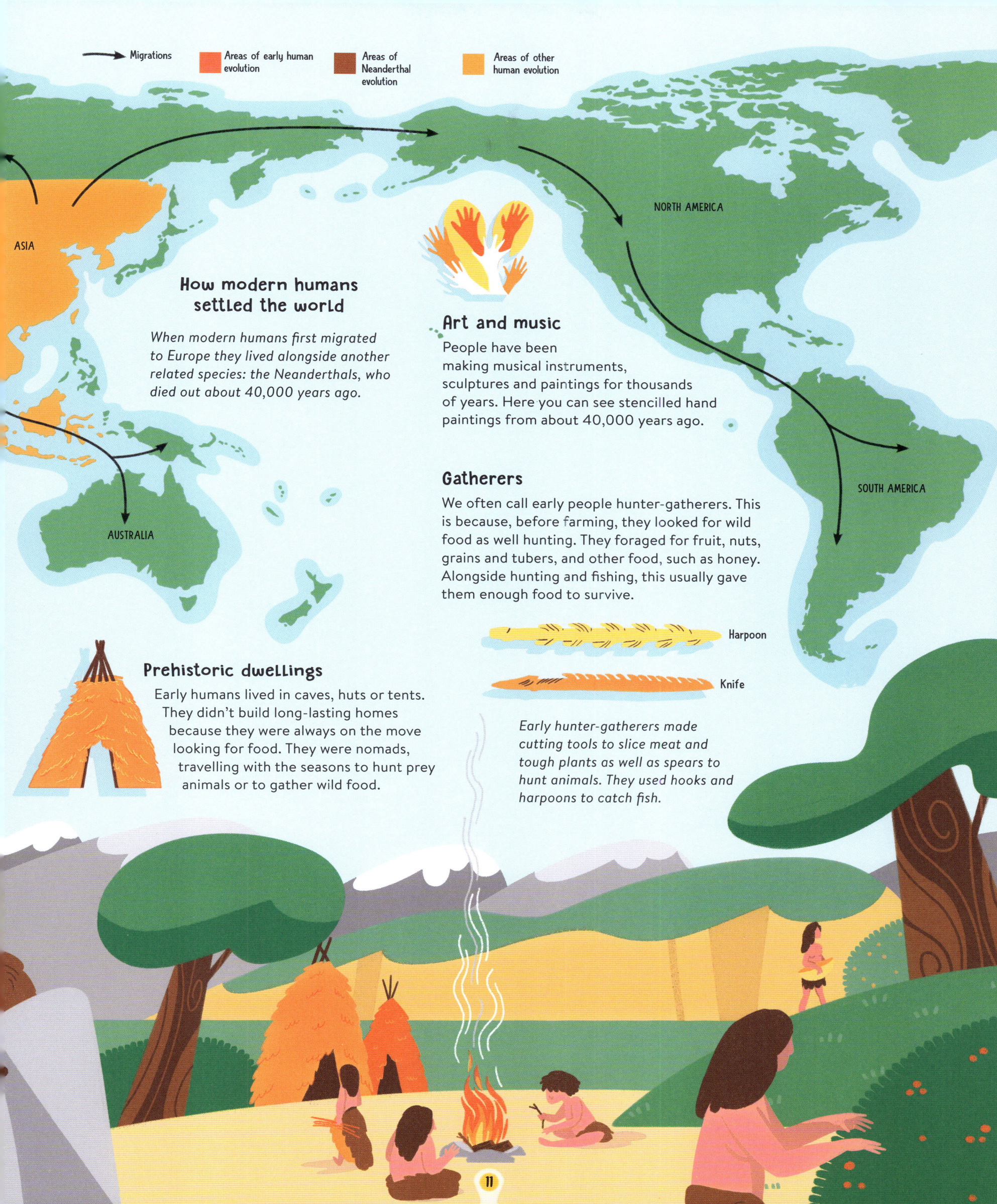

→ Migrations   ▭ Areas of early human evolution   ▭ Areas of Neanderthal evolution   ▭ Areas of other human evolution

How modern humans settled the world

When modern humans first migrated to Europe they lived alongside another related species: the Neanderthals, who died out about 40,000 years ago.

Art and music

People have been making musical instruments, sculptures and paintings for thousands of years. Here you can see stencilled hand paintings from about 40,000 years ago.

Gatherers

We often call early people hunter-gatherers. This is because, before farming, they looked for wild food as well hunting. They foraged for fruit, nuts, grains and tubers, and other food, such as honey. Alongside hunting and fishing, this usually gave them enough food to survive.

Harpoon

Knife

Early hunter-gatherers made cutting tools to slice meat and tough plants as well as spears to hunt animals. They used hooks and harpoons to catch fish.

Prehistoric dwellings

Early humans lived in caves, huts or tents. They didn't build long-lasting homes because they were always on the move looking for food. They were nomads, travelling with the seasons to hunt prey animals or to gather wild food.

THE BIRTH OF FARMING

Over thousands of years, nomadic hunter-gatherers became settled farmers. They grew plants for food rather than foraging. They also raised animals, such as chickens, pigs and goats. This late Stone Age era is called the Neolithic. People still used stone tools but everyday life was changing.

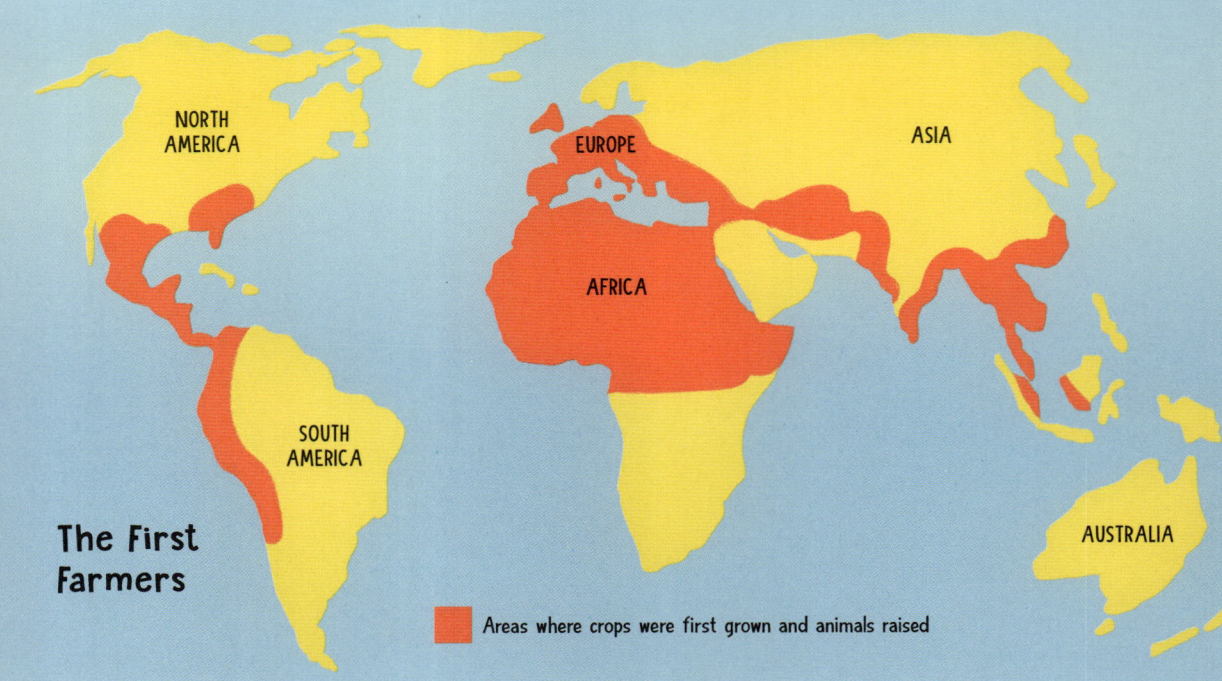

The First Farmers

■ Areas where crops were first grown and animals raised

Music, art and writing

Neolithic art consisted mostly of pottery, terracotta sculptures, small statues, wall paintings (some just patterns and others more lifelike), and huge stone monuments. People made music to accompany their ceremonies and to dance to. At the end of prehistory, people invented writing systems to record their activities and ideas.

Musical instruments included drums, horns, flutes and rattles. This is a goatskin drum.

From village to town

Early farmers lived together in small villages, which they defended with walls. Each family had its own house, but they shared things such as meeting halls and pottery kilns. With more available food from farming, villages very slowly grew into towns and cities.

Defensive walls

Milking a goat

Venus figures

Before the Neolithic era, people carved small statues of women. They were possibly a symbol of their religious beliefs.

These small figures have been found in Europe and Asia. They are named after Venus, the Roman goddess of love.

Monument building

Around 6,500 years ago, people began building monuments using huge stones called megaliths. The first monuments were used as tombs for groups of people. Later, some megaliths were arranged in circles and perhaps used to celebrate the harvest and the seasons.

Dolmens were tombs made of megaliths (stones), with upright stones holding up a single top stone. Some dolmens were covered with more stones and earth.

Humans first domesticated pigs about 9,000 years ago.

Goats were domesticated about 10,000 years ago.

Raising animals

Humans began raising animals by domesticating them. They caught the animals from the wild and bred from them. These domesticated animals gave milk, meat and eggs to eat, and hides and wool for clothing. They were also used to carry or pull heavy loads.

Pottery

Clay pots are heavy and easily broken, so pottery only became widespread when people settled in villages. They invented potter's wheels to make pots more easily and kilns to bake (or fire) them hard.

The change from living as nomadic hunter-gatherers to settled farmers was gradual but without it human civilisations would not have developed.

Making pottery

Weaving

Cooking

Grinding grain into flour

This copper art found in Israel was made around 3500 BCE.

Metalwork

Learning how to work metal was another change that led to the development of human civilisation. Copper was the first metal people used, from about 10,000 years ago. They found this soft metal as nuggets in rocks and beat it into shape for use as tools and ornaments. Around 5000 BCE, people discovered how to smelt copper and extract it from its ore.

Metal was smelted in huge stone pots.

Crops

Early farmers planted the seeds of wild cereals such as wheat and barley (in Western Asia), rice and millet (in Eastern Asia), maize (in Central and South America) and sorghum (in Africa). Figs and other fruits and vegetables were also grown.

Sickles and scythes were used to harvest cereals, while adzes were used to hoe the soil and chop things.

An adze, for hoeing and chopping

Farming tools

Early farmers used pointed digging sticks to prepare the ground for sewing seeds. The first wooden ploughs were used to turn the soil about 6,500 years ago. Later, a metal blade was added to the plough which cut deeper into the hard ground.

A scythe and a sickle, for harvesting grains

A hand mill, for grinding grain into flour

Ancient Egypt is Africa's earliest and most famous civilisation, but there were many others. Some developed around the same time as Egypt, like the Land of Punt, but others grew up much later, such as the Kingdom of Benin. We can learn a lot about them from the ruins of their cities and the amazing art they left behind.

The Nile Valley

- Pyramids of Giza
- Sphinx
- Saqqara – with a step pyramid
- Valley of the Kings – Tutankhamun buried here
- Temple of Karnak
- Temple of Luxor
- Temple of Abu Simbel
- River Nile
- Red Sea

ANCIENT EGYPT

The ancient Egyptians lived along the banks of the River Nile and their lives centred around it. Each year the river flooded, covering the land either side of it with a thick layer of fertile, black mud in which the Egyptians grew their crops. They called the river valley *kemet*, 'the black land', and themselves *remet-en-kemet*, 'the people of the black land'. The Bronze Age kingdom of Egypt first came together around 3100 BCE and lasted for almost 3,000 years. It was one of the longest civiliastions ever known.

The Pharaoh

The Egyptian king, or 'pharaoh' was all powerful and his people believed he was a living god. He was head of the government and the army.

Amun | Khnum | Maat | Isis | Osiris | Horus | Hathor | Sekhmet | Seth | Sobek | Taweret

Above: The Egyptians had many gods and goddesses. Some, such as Osiris, Horus and Isis, were worshipped all over Egypt; others were local gods.

Scribes and writing

The Egyptians were among the first people to invent a system of writing. They used picture-like hieroglyphs. Only a few people, called scribes, could read and write. Scribes kept records, not only of taxes and harvests, but also of daily life and historic events.

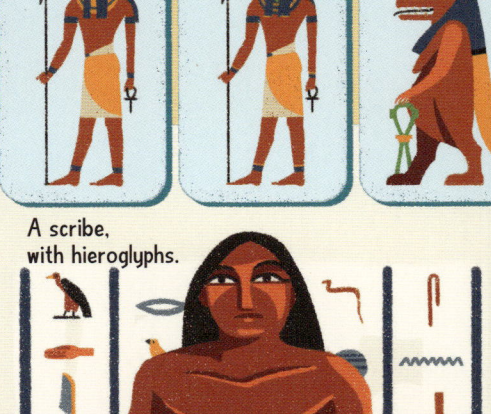

A scribe, with hieroglyphs.

The festival of Opet

The Egyptian year was full of religious celebrations and feast days. At the festival of Opet, priests took the statue of the god Amun from the temple at Karnak and carried it downriver to the temple at Luxor.

Pyramids

During a time known as the Old Kingdom (c. 2700–2200 BCE), the Egyptians built pyramids as tombs for their pharaohs. The most famous are at Giza.

The Great Pyramid at Giza is the largest of the pyramids. It was built 4,500 years ago and still stands today.

The Great Sphinx was brightly coloured when it was first made. Today, its colours have faded.

The Great Sphinx

In front of the pyramids at Giza is a huge statue of the Sphinx, a mythical creature with the body of a lion and the head of a man.

Later, pharaohs were buried in underground tombs, especially in a place now known as the Valley of the Kings.

Weighing of the heart

The Egyptians believed that when a person died they went to an afterlife. During the Weighing of the Heart, a priest wearing the mask of Anubis weighed the dead person's heart on a scale balanced against a feather. If it balanced, the dead person would travel safely to the afterlife.

Preserving the body

The Egyptians thought that a dead person's body should be preserved as a mummy, ready for the afterlife. Priests took out the insides from a dead body, filled it with special salts and wrapped it in pieces of linen. The rich were placed in ornate mummy cases.

Mummy case with mummy inside

Farming and daily life

Most people in Egypt were farmers. They worked the land, growing wheat and barley for bread and beer, and grapes for wine. Others were slaves or worked as soldiers, craftspeople, merchants, priests and scribes.

Music and entertainment

People enjoyed religious festivals and private parties. The wealthy could afford to hire musicians and dancers to perform. They held banquets where the women wore their best jewellery and put perfumed beeswax in their hair.

African Civilisations

This map shows where some of the ancient African cultures were found.

ANCIENT AFRICA

There were many African civilisations. Some developed during the Egyptian era, such as Kush and Aksum. Others came much later, such as Benin, who still ruled in West Africa when European settlers took control of their lands. These civilisations traded with each other across Africa and into Europe and Asia. There was plenty of exchange of ideas and religious beliefs, but they each had their own unique culture.

The Land of Punt

The Egyptians traded with Punt, a land which probably lay to their south-east. This civilisation flourished from c. 2500–980 BCE. It was known for its precious gold, ivory and incense. The Egyptians also bought wild animals from them.

On some of their wall paintings, the Egyptians showed the people of Punt bringing gifts.

Aksum pillar, or stele (right), and a coin (below).

Aksum

This kingdom existed between 150 BCE and 960 CE. It linked trade between Europe and India. Aksum developed a writing system called the Ge'ez script. It became Christian around 324 CE.

The kingdom of Kush

Lasting from around 1050 BCE to 550 CE, this kingdom was centred in Nubia, south of Egypt, on the Nile. At one point, the Kushites controlled all of Egypt. Despite Egyptian influences, the Kushite culture was strong with its own language and writing systems. Women were very important, both in politics and religion.

The Kushite kings and queens were buried in small pyramids at Meroe, its capital from c. 600 BCE.

The Ghana Empire

This desert civilisation dominated areas of Saharan West Africa from around 300 to 1200 CE. The empire was built thanks to its success in trading in gold and salt across the Sahara desert. This trade had existed for centuries but it grew with the arrival of the camel. The modern country of Ghana is in a different part of Africa but is named in honour of this ancient empire.

Camels survive well in the desert. They were introduced to the western Sahara from Egypt and the Middle East in the 4th century CE. Soon caravans of camels carried precious goods across the Sahara.

The clay used for Nok figures came from one source, perhaps controlled by royalty.

Nok culture

Around the 4th century BCE, a civilisation emerged in West Africa south of the Sahara. It is known for its amazing clay sculptures of human heads and figures. These figures were first rediscoverd around Nok in modern Nigeria, giving the culture its name.

Iron ore was smelted in furnaces. Once the iron was extracted, it was shaped into tools over hot fires laid in stone basins.

Metal workers

The Nok were the first people in this region to create clay figures. They were also the first to smelt iron to make tools and weapons. Unlike many civilisations, including the Egyptians, they never worked with bronze but went straight to the Iron Age. With metal tools, they were able to improve farming methods. Their crops included sorghum and pumpkins.

The Great Enclosure in the city had walls over 10 metres high. It was probably where the royal family lived.

Great Zimbabwe

This stone city was built in the 11th century CE by the ancestors of the Shona people of modern Zimbabwe, giving the country its name. 'Zimbabwe' means 'stone houses' in Shona. The city lay at the centre of the Kingdom of Zimbabwe, a civilisation that grew out of the rich trade around southern Africa and with the rest of the world. The city was abandoned in the 15th century.

In total Great Zimbabwe is thought to have been home to around 10,000 people.

Royal compound — Thatched houses — Defensive walls

The Kingdom of Benin

This West African kingdom emerged in the 12th century CE and continued until Britain made it part of its empire in 1897. In the 15th century, Benin traded with the Portuguese, whose boats stopped in their harbours, and later with other Europeans. Its artists are famous for their sculptures (often made of brass) of people and historic events.

A 16th century head of Queen Idia of Benin. Mother of the King, Idia was said to be a great warrior.

The world's earliest civilisations arose in the river valleys of Asia. The Sumerians built some of the first cities between the Tigris and the Euphrates rivers in Mesopotamia. Chinese civilisation began along the Yellow and Yangtze rivers, while the first city-based cultures in South Asia began in the Indus River valley.

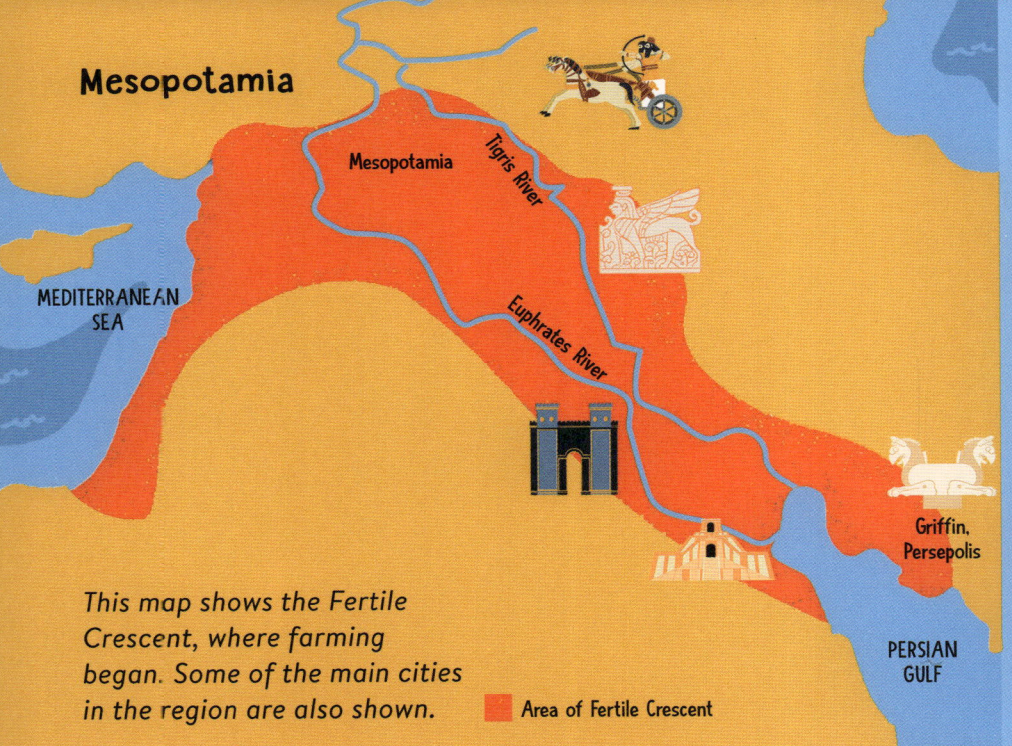

Mesopotamia

This map shows the Fertile Crescent, where farming began. Some of the main cities in the region are also shown.

■ Area of Fertile Crescent

MESOPOTAMIA

People began to settle and farm the fertile land in the hills above the Tigris and Euphrates rivers more than 15,000 years ago. Around 6000 BCE, as irrigation techniques developed, people moved into the lands between these two rivers (Mesopotamia in ancient Greek), now modern Iraq. They built the some of the first cities. Some 2,500 years later, the Bronze Age Sumerians settled here and made many key developments. They were the first to use the wheel, invented a writing system based on sounds, and started the sciences of maths and astronomy.

Daily Life and trade

Much of life focused around food: from farming to fishing, as shown in some Sumerian art (above). In the cities there were markets and workshops. Different cities prospered at different times. Each city and the area its people controlled had their own culture and identity, and were often later described as city-states, or even civilisations in their own right. They sold goods along the trade routes east to India and China, and west to the Mediterranean, reaching both ancient Egypt and the Indus Valley. These trading ties affected how their cultures developed.

The birth of writing

Around 3,300 BCE, some people in Mesopotamia started using a pictogram script which is known as 'proto-cuneiform'. Over hundreds of years, this developed into 'cuneiform', the written form of the Sumerian language. It used symbols to show sounds rather than things, allowing it to be later adapted to other languages. As states grew up around cities, their rulers could write laws, record taxes and keep their histories.

Proto-cuneiform and later cuneiform were written on clay tablets.

Pottery

Pottery techniques developed in Mesopotamia. The Sumerians knew how to shape clay on a wheel and fire it hard in a kiln (a type of oven). This let people make pottery faster, and busy workshops grew up. The potter's wheel led to another development: using the wheel for transport.

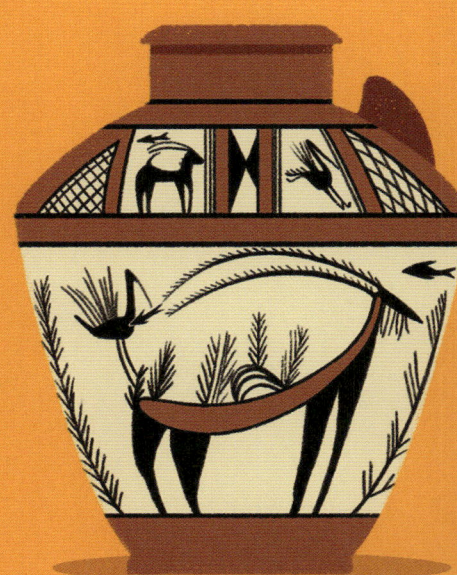

By 2,800 BCE, the Sumerians were making beautiful, decorated pots like this one.

Women's Lives

People's lives changed over the thousands of years of Mesopotamia's civilisations. Women's lives mainly focused on the home, marriage and children. However, from cuneiform tablets, we know women worked as well – for example, as scribes, artists, farmers and bakers. There were powerful royal women and priestesses. Richer women could own land and businesses. Others had harder lives as servants and slaves.

Sumerian royal women wore jewellery like this dating from 2,600–2,400 BCE.

Men's Lives

Men mostly controlled Mesopotamian cities and their states, from kings and generals to scribes and tax collectors. Richer boys went to school, but others learnt a trade in workshops or worked on farms. Many were servants and slaves. Most men were expected to fight for their city, although later there were also professional soldiers.

Weapons and warfare

The first war ever recorded took place in Mesopotamia (c. 2,700 BCE). The city-states often fought each other. Their armies had powerful weapons, such as axes and spears, made with their increasing skill in metalwork, using bronze and, later, iron.

The wheel

The Sumerians first used wheels in carts that were heavy and slow. The Assyrians, another Mesopotamian people, later developed much lighter wheels for their fast war chariots. These chariots helped them build an empire (911–609 BCE) across much of West Asia.

An Assyrian war chariot as seen on the wall of Nineveh, one of Assyria's great cities.

Following the sun and stars

The Mesopotamians worshipped many gods, including the god of the sun, shown here greeting a king. To follow the sun and map the stars, they developed maths to measure angles, based on 360° in a circle. They measured time, too, using seconds, minutes and hours for the first time.

Shamash, the sun god

Building to the heavens

The Mesopotamians built massive, stepped buildings called ziggurats. Part of a temple complex, a ziggurat was home to the gods and only priests and the king were allowed into it. Ordinary people worshipped in temples next to the ziggurat and left statues of themselves as gifts for the gods.

The Ziggurat of Ur (started c. 2,050 BCE)

Amazing stories

The Mesopotamians told wonderful stories about gods and heroes, such as Gilgamesh. Their tales of the Great Flood inspired the story of the flood and Noah's Ark in the Hebrew Bible.

This image from the walls of Nineveh shows a god fighting a griffin.

Ancient Persia

The last great civilisation of ancient Mesopotamia was led by the Persians, who built a city at Persepolis (started c. 510 BCE). Their huge empire was taken over by the Greeks in 330 BCE.

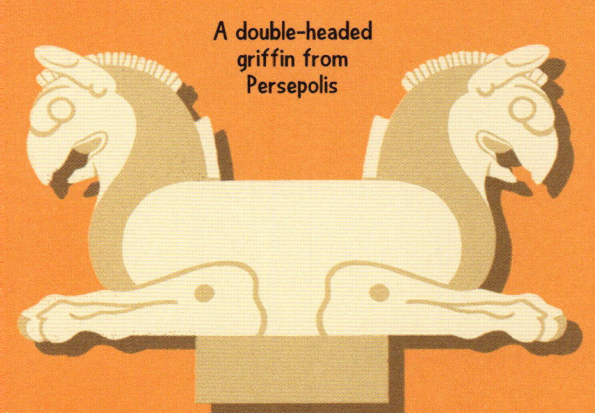

A double-headed griffin from Persepolis

THE INDUS VALLEY

A civilisation grew up in the Indus River Valley about 5,000 years ago. Its wealth was based on agriculture and trade. Farmers grew crops along the Indus River's fertile banks. The two main cities were Mohenjo-Daro and Harappa, which were well-planned and efficiently run. The Indus Valley people, also known as Harappans, had systems of counting, measuring, weighing and writing, although today no one can understand their script. Their culture may have contributed to later Indian civilisations.

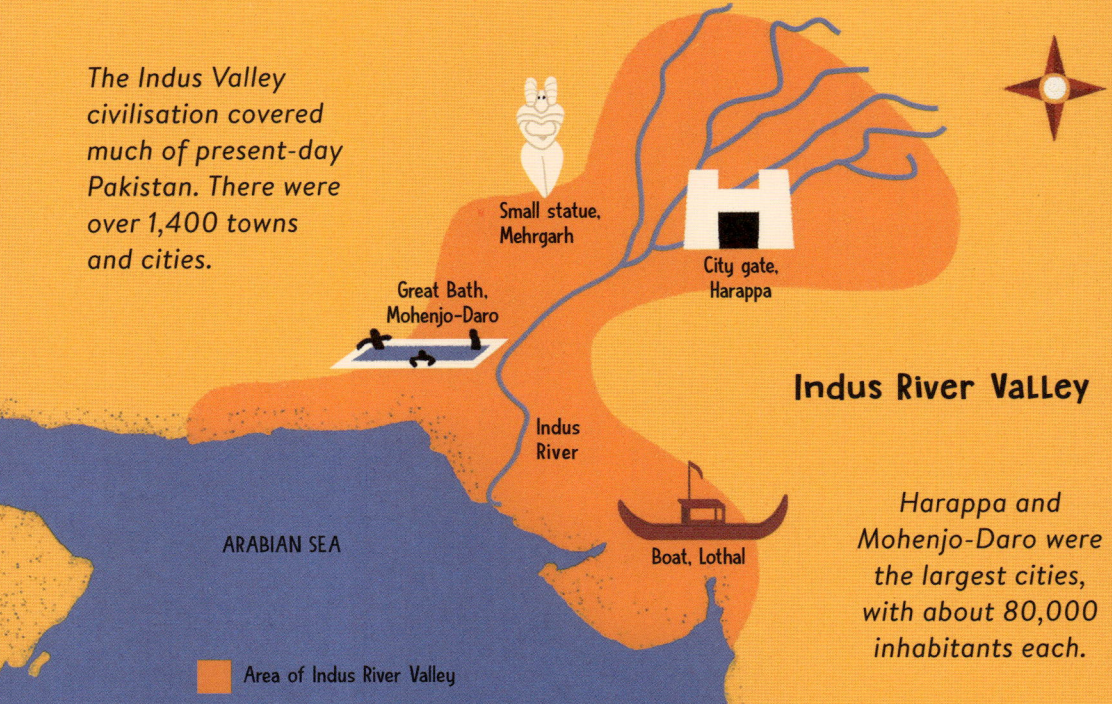

The Indus Valley civilisation covered much of present-day Pakistan. There were over 1,400 towns and cities.

Indus River Valley

Harappa and Mohenjo-Daro were the largest cities, with about 80,000 inhabitants each.

Who were they?

The Indus Valley people were the descendants of local hunter-gatherers. By 6,000 BCE they were farming the fertile land along the river banks.

Small terracotta statues of women wearing chunky jewellery were popular.

Trade

The Harappans traded widely, bartering (exchanging) goods as far afield as Mesopotamia, Persia and Central Asia. They exported cotton, beads, tools and weapons in exchange for grain, metals (like gold and silver) and gemstones (such as lapis lazuli and turquoise).

A balance scale and weights. The Harappans had standard weights and measures which worked like grams and kilograms.

Clothes

Clothes were generally made of cotton, but linen, wool, silk and leather were also used. Both men and women wore jewellery made of gold, silver or copper and decorated with precious stones.

Daily Life

Most people lived as farmers, but there were also masons and craftsmen to build houses and make furniture. Artists and jewellers made sculptures, necklaces and other things of beauty.

Examples of Indus writing symbols

Seals and writing

About 3,500 small stone seals have been found. They are decorated with pictures of animals, including bulls, unicorns, elephants and rhinoceroses. They all have inscriptions, but experts have not been able work out what they mean. Similar markings have been found on pots. About 400 different symbols have been found. The seals were probably used as tags to identify goods or the people selling them.

Bull seal | Unicorn seal | Rhino seal | Elephant seal

Cities and houses

Cities were divided into a lower town where most people lived. A higher, walled citadel, was home to the rulers. It had warehouses for storing grain and public baths. Streets in the lower town were laid out in a neat criss-cross pattern. The houses were built from kiln-baked mud bricks. They had a single entrance door and a central courtyard, often with a well for fresh water. Many had indoor bathrooms with pipes connected to drains under the city streets.

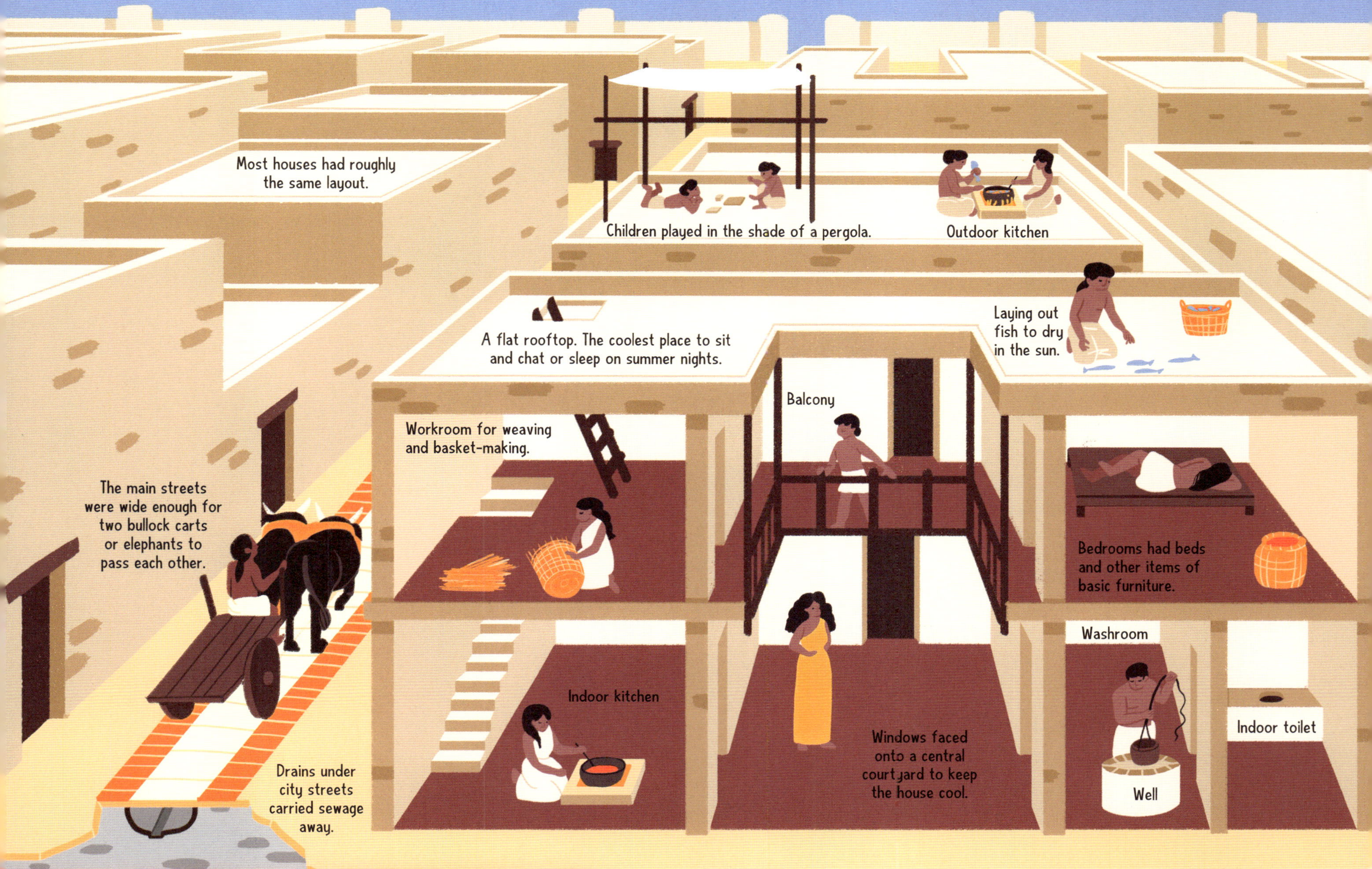

Most houses had roughly the same layout.

Children played in the shade of a pergola.

Outdoor kitchen

A flat rooftop. The coolest place to sit and chat or sleep on summer nights.

Laying out fish to dry in the sun.

Balcony

Workroom for weaving and basket-making.

Bedrooms had beds and other items of basic furniture.

The main streets were wide enough for two bullock carts or elephants to pass each other.

Indoor kitchen

Windows faced onto a central courtyard to keep the house cool.

Washroom

Well

Indoor toilet

Drains under city streets carried sewage away.

Who ruled?

We don't know how the Indus Valley civilisation was governed, but society was complex and well-organised so there must have been some form of political control. It may have been a monarchy led by kings and queens. Or perhaps a group of powerful citizens, or priests, oversaw things.

This soapstone figurine of a bearded king or priest was found in the ruins of Mohenjo-Daro.

Coming to an end

Harappan civilisation declined gradually over many years. By 1,700 BCE most of the big cities had been abandoned. Archaeologists think that it was caused by climate change as the region became cooler and drier. A long drought and unpredictable floods made farming difficult.

Some experts believe that the decline was caused by the collapse of trading links with Mesopotamia.

According to another theory, invaders destroyed this civilisation.

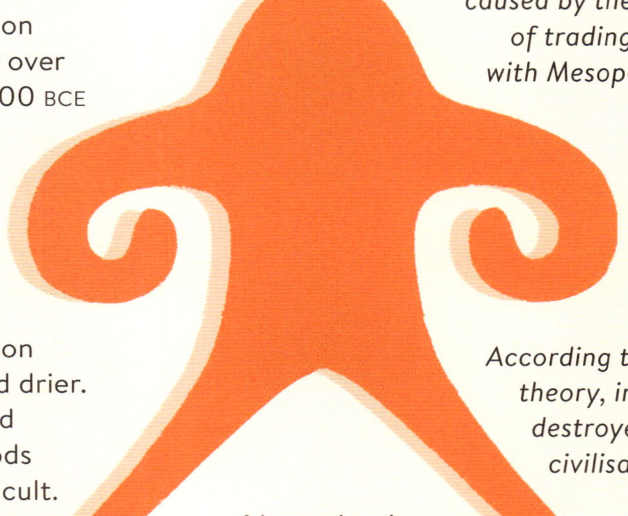

A human-shaped copper figure from the Indus Valley

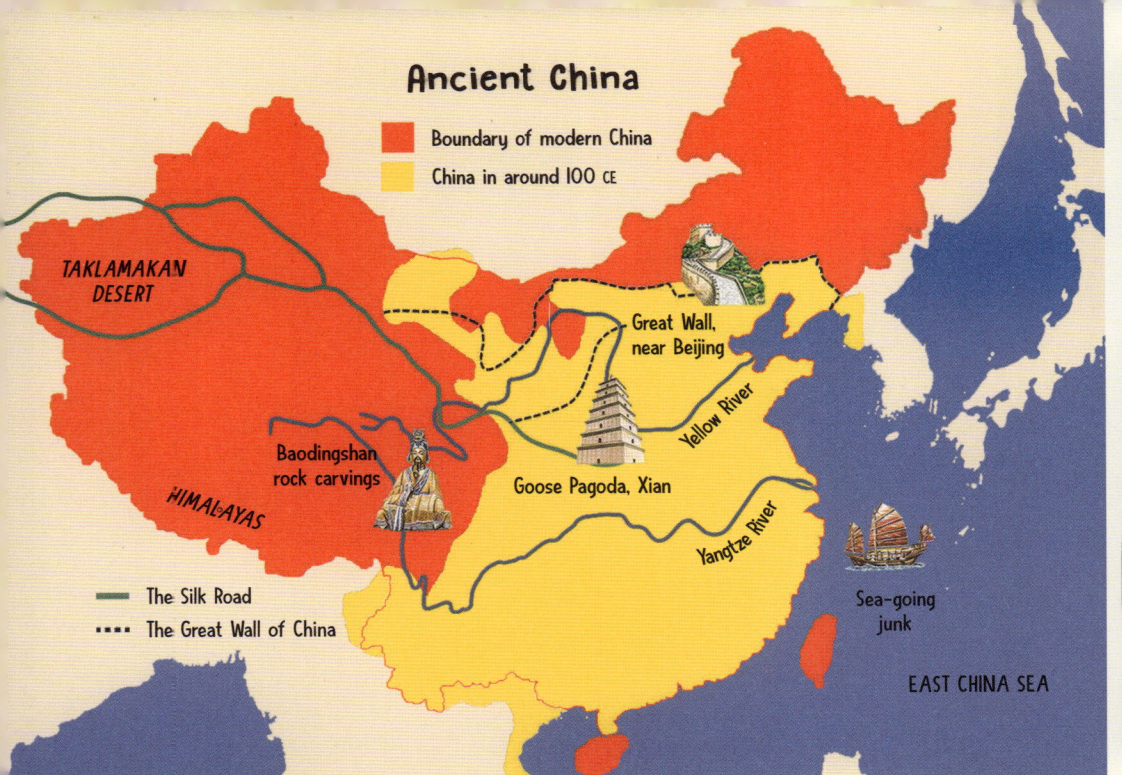

Ancient China

- Boundary of modern China
- China in around 100 CE

TAKLAMAKAN DESERT
Great Wall, near Beijing
Baodingshan rock carvings
Goose Pagoda, Xian
Yellow River
Yangtze River
HIMALAYAS
Sea-going junk
EAST CHINA SEA

— The Silk Road
---- The Great Wall of China

ANCIENT CHINA

China is one of the oldest civilisations in the world. Like others, it grew from a few riverside farming villages over 8,000 years ago. By the Yellow River in the north, the Chinese grew millet. Along the Yangtze River to the south, rice was the main crop. As the population increased, fights broke out between rival leaders and people moved into walled villages for safety. These villages grew into towns and then cities, ruled by powerful leaders and their families. These families became known as dynasties. The last dynasty to rule China ended in 1911 CE, just over a hundred years ago.

From its origins in the area between the Yellow and Yangtze Rivers, ancient China gradually grew and spread west as new lands were conquered.

Early art and writing

By 4,000 BCE, Chinese villagers were making beautiful pottery, some of it using a wheel. They also made stone tools and ornaments. Objects carved from hard, green jade were particularly precious. The villagers traded with other communities.

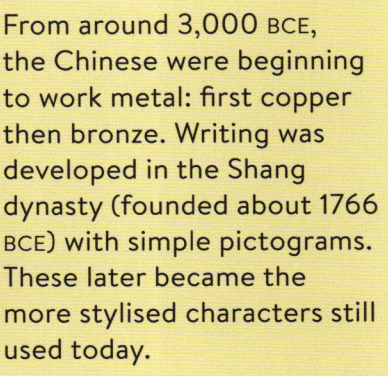

From around 3,000 BCE, the Chinese were beginning to work metal: first copper then bronze. Writing was developed in the Shang dynasty (founded about 1766 BCE) with simple pictograms. These later became the more stylised characters still used today.

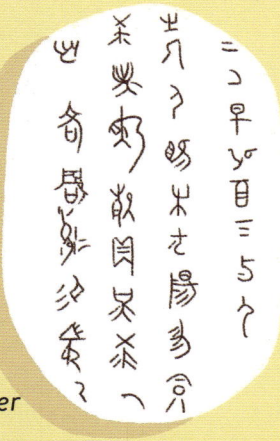

Early Chinese pictograms carved on a tortoise shell.

A storage vessel from a Yellow River Neolithic farming community.

Beliefs – the three ways

Three religions took root in China. the first was Confucianism, named after Confucius (551–479 BCE). A rival religion, Taoism, grew up from the 4th century BCE. About 100 CE Buddhism from India spread in China.

Confucius taught the importance of kindness and respect for the family.

Taoism was based on the teachings of Laozi, who also lived about 500 BCE.

Buddha lived in India around the same time as Confucius.

Buried with an army

The first emperor, Qin Shi Huang, died in 210 BCE. He was buried in a great tomb with his own army made of terracotta clay beside him. There were over 8,000 life-size, clay soldiers.

Two figures of archers from the Terracotta Army.

The Empress Wu Zetian was a wise and effective leader during the Tang dynasty (628–907 CE). She was the only woman ever to rule China as emperor.

Dynasties and emperors

Legends tell of Chinese dynasties from about 2,500 BCE, but the Shang dynasty is the first to leave historical records. It controlled parts of China for about 600 years. When the leader of the Qin dynasty, Qin Shi Huang, united China in 221 BCE, he declared himself emperor.

The Great Wall

The Great Wall of China is about 2,400 km long. It began as a series of earth banks built to keep out invaders from the north. Qin Shi Huang connected them up when he united China. The structure seen today dates from the 16th century.

The Great Wall not only protected China but was also used to control and tax trade along the Silk Road.

Silk cocoons were boiled and their silk-thread casing was spun and woven into cloth.

Inventions

The Chinese were great innovators and inventors. As early as 4,000 BCE they discovered how to make silk from the cocoons of moths. They invented paper (in 105 CE according to Chinese records) and then developed techniques to print on it. Sometime before 1000 CE they invented gunpower and around the 11th century CE they used a magnetic compass.

The first compasses used a natural magnet called a lodestone.

A porcelain vase

The arts

Chinese civilisation has a rich tradition of creativity, including art and poetry, often linked by calligraphy (the art of writing). Calligraphers worked in ink and watercolour on scrolls. Artists created amazing objects, such as the early cast bronze vessels and later porcelain 'china' so fine you could see through it. Music too was important from earliest times and a unique form of opera developed.

The Monkey King from a Chinese opera, based on a famous 16th century CE novel.

The Silk Road and trade

By the 2nd century BCE, the Silk Road connected China to West Asia and Europe. It was a trade route, named after Chinese silk, the most precious of the many goods that were carried and sold along it. Later, Chinese porcelain pottery was exported to the West by sea. It was prized for its delicacy and beautiful decorations.

Ancient Korea – the Three Kingdoms

The Three Kingdoms were Silla, Baekje and Goguryeo. Gaya was an area of small cities with no overall king.

ANCIENT KOREA

People first settled on the Korean peninsula over 12,000 years ago. Its position next to China meant Korea always had links with China, but Korea developed its own unique civilisation and culture. An important time for this was the Three Kingdom Period (57 BCE–688 CE), when the area was, in fact, divided into four different states. Later unified, another key period was the Goryeo dynasty (918–1392 CE).

The first decorated pottery found in Korea dates back to around 7000 BCE.

Traditional clothes

During the Three Kingdom Period, Koreans developed a form of traditional dress called 'hanbok'. Designed for ease of movement, it was widely worn for over 2,000 years.

Hanbok outfits were made up of a top, trousers or a skirt, with a long coat or jacket over the top.

Bronze coins from the Goryeo dynasty

Relationship with China

From the earliest times, Korean links with China were strong. They sometimes fought against each other, but they also traded together. Koreans adopted and adapted Chinese ideas ranging from coinage to education.

Korea first minted its own coins in the Goryeo era. Chinese coins were often used before that.

Writing and printing

The Koreans adopted Chinese characters to write during the Three Kingdom Period. They also used Chinese printing techniques, but took them further. They invented moveable metal type, some 78 years before it was used in Europe to print the Gutenberg Bible. The oldest book in the world printed using this technology is Jikji from 1377.

Jikji is a book of Buddhist sayings.

Science and technology

The Koreans made advances in science and technology too. In astronomy, they built the oldest known observatory tower in 647 CE. In maths, the Goryeo dynasty developed a way of recording trade in a business called 'double-entry book-keeping', where you see money going in and coming out at the same time. This was at least 100 years before a similar system was developed in Europe.

Over 9 metres tall, the Cheomseongdae observatory was built in Silla to watch the stars.

A traditional Korean masked dancer

Stone temples
As part of their Buddhist beliefs, the ancient Koreans built pagoda temples, with steep layered roofs. Some pagodas were built of stone. The Koreans cleverly adapted woodworking techniques to create these unique buildings.

Mireuksaji Stone Pagoda (639 CE)

Beliefs
The early Koreans worshipped many gods through nature and the spirit world. Buddhism reached them via China and it became the main religion from the 4th century CE. Some of the older traditions continued.

Celadon pots
Korea learnt some of their pottery skills from the Chinese but developed them to a very high standard. Green glazed celadon ware was so prized it was exported back to China.

A Celadon pot (12th century CE)

The owner of this folk art painting hoped for long life, as symbolised by the animals and landscape.

Folk art
There was a tradition of folk art in Korea. Travelling artists with no formal training painted these images, often of animals, to sell. They were meant to bring good luck.

Education
Influenced by Chinese Confucianism and Buddhism, the Koreans introduced a form of state education during the Three Kingdom Period. Only boys from wealthy backgrounds went to school.

Education was highly prized in Korea. To take a role in running the country, boys had to pass an exam, which was first introduced 788 CE and continued until 1894.

Structure of society
The Koreans had a very structured society. At the top was the king, surrounded by a ruling group of male landowners. Next were peasant farmers, who usually owned some land. They paid tax to the state. Lower still were slave labourers, who were often the children of slaves. Women, from whatever group, had little power and stayed largely in the home.

In 1443, King Sejong the Great created hangul, a Korean script still used today. He aimed to make it easier to learn to read and write.

ANCIENT JAPAN

People first crossed from the Asian mainland to Japan about 40,000 years ago. There were further migrations from China and Korea in the centuries that followed. In legend, Japan's first emperor was Jimmu, who led the country from 660 BCE, but historians only wrote about him about 1,000 years later. Influenced by ideas from China and Korea, Japan's civilisation grew rapidly from around 300 CE as its many small kingdoms became united under one ruler.

This map of Japan shows its four main islands and some of its key cities in 750 CE.

Pottery
Ancient Japanese pottery dates back to 14,500 BCE – the oldest in the world. Known as 'Jomon', these pots give their name to this early Japanese culture.

Jomon ware is named after the cords that its makers pressed into the clay to decorate it.

Storytelling
Storytelling has a rich tradition in Japan. *The Tale of Genji*, written by Murasaki Shikibu in 11th century CE, is often said to be the first novel.

Murasaki Shikibu, shown writing here, was a lady-in-waiting to the Empress.

Writing system
The Japanese were writing with Chinese characters by the 4th century CE. They gradually adapted these to express their own language and developed their own writing stystem.

Sakura – cherry blossom | Love | Fox | Japan | Moon | Fire

Farming
People began farming in Japan around 5,000 BCE. Rice, introduced from mainland Asia, was grown from around 600 BCE. Surrounded by the sea, fish was a key part of Japan's diet.

Farmers carried their produce to market on poles.

Emperors and government
The ancient Japanese were ruled by Emperors and Empresses. By the 7th century CE, they worked with a system similar to China, built up by Prince Shotoku (who ruled on behalf on the Empress Suiko). It was centred on the imperial family, and all taxes were paid to them, but it was run by educated officials.

Prince Shotoku (574-622 CE) is seen as one of Japan's great rulers.